EUGENE J. MCCARTHY

SELECTED POEMS

"Terra Terribilia"

The ancient mapmakers used the term
"terra terribilia" to identify what was beyond
their knowledge of the earth. A notation
on one of these maps described the "terra
terribilia" in these words:

> "All beyond is nothing
> but dry and desert sands,
> inhabited only by wild creatures
> or dark impassable bogs,
> of Scythian cold
> or frozen sea,
> beyond which there is nothing
> but monstrous and tragical fiction.
> There the poets and inventors of fables dwell."

This book is a tribute to American poets
like Robert Lowell, William Stafford, Robert Bly,
Reed Whittemore, James Dickey, Philip Booth,   ·
and the many others who have written of
this country and of its people; to poets
who have gone beyond the "known" and the
"certain" into the "terra terribilia" in the
search for truth.

Eugene J. McCarthy

Selected Poems

Published
by
Lone Oak Press
304 11th Avenue Southeast
Rochester, Minnesota 55904

ISBN 1-883477-15-8
Library of Congress
Catalog Card Number: 96-080054

Contents

The Book of Yeats

A Book of Yeats, she gave to me.
"Read this," she said, and think no more of you and me.

I sat and read, and read,
with bowed head,
while the waiting years
rustled at my ears,
shoving and pushing for a place
upon my narrow shoulder blades,
like vultures on too small a branch.

And then I said,
"We who together the great gazebo built
and struck the match and blew the flame
to burn time down
will live on now in curtained rooms
and let time grow as rank
as tamarack in a swamp,
all green below while dying at the top.

"And we who watched the moon stagger
across the sky
and drank its mad light and danced
to all its phases
will come on dark nights, alone,
when only owls can see and blind moles
mate and move.

"And we who together laughed at Anne Gregory's hair
and changed its color to our own desire
will think no more of chestnut or of yellow,
or laugh together, or new texts contrive.

"And we who played
you the trout turned
glimmering girl,
and I the Aengus
following, desperate,
through hollow and through hilly lands,
the chase ending at last
in long dappled grass
will walk only in flat places,
separate, yet within each other's sight,
like fixed stars, in a parking lot,
our light slowly dying.

"And we who heard the curlew ..."

"Put down the book," she cried.
"Give me your hand and rest
your head upon my breast."

Then all the bare-necked birds
flew off my back.

The Needed Word

Always it is there
And then lost.
Between the night and the veil
Of whitening morning light
And then again
In the shadows of dusk.

We pursue it,
Riding pale horses
Among the aspen trees.
Or as rider and ridden,
Last centaurs among
Elm and oak.

We seek it as diggers
In one more cave,
Where bats flutter
And hang upside down.
Seeking the one last gospel,
Not found,
Seeking the needed word,
Needed.

The Death Of The Old Plymouth Rock Hen

It was tragic when her time came
After a lifetime of laying brown eggs
Among the white of leghorns.
Now, unattractive to the rooster,
Laying no more eggs,
Faking it on other hens' nests,
Caught in the act,
Taken to the woodpile
In the winter of execution.

A quick stroke of the axe,
One first and last upward cast
Of eyes that in life
Had looked only down,
Scanning the ground for seeds and worms
And for the shadow of the hawk.
Now those eyes are covered
By yellow lids,
Closing from the bottom up.

Decapitated, she did not act
Like a chicken with its head cut off.
No pirouettes, no somersaults,
No last indignity.
Like an English queen, she died.
On wings that had never known flight
She flew, straight into the woodpile,
And there beat out slow death
While her curdled voice ran out in blood.

A scalding and a plucking of no purpose.
No goose feathers for a comforter.
No duck's down for a pillow.
No quill for a pen.
In the opened body, no entrail message for the haruspex.
Not one egg of promise in the oviduct.
In the gray gizzard, no diamond or emerald,
But only half-ground corn,
Sure evidence of unprofitability.

The breast and legs,
The wings and things,
The strong heart,
The pope's nose,
Fit only for chicken soup and stew.
And then in March, near winter's end,
When blooded and feathered wood is used,
The odor of burnt offerings
Above the kitchen stove.

Three Poems About Cows

Marc Chagall

When I met Marc Chagall
I asked him first of all
whether he had ever seen
in life or in a dream
a cow just sitting down.
He said that he had seen
cows both blue and green
and also that he knew
cows that danced and cows that flew
but that he had never seen
in life or in a dream
a cow just sitting down.

The Cow

The cow is a very strange beast.
Because of missing upper teeth
it cannot bite or eat directly,
therefore it ruminates.
It has several stomachs.
When it lies down
it does one half at a time,
first the front, then the rear.
When it gets up
it does the reverse,
first the rear, then the front.
Since this is its way
a cow never voluntarily sits down.

Moon Shot
Dedicated to the Manned Spacecraft Center

There once was a cow.
Do not ask how
but when bit by a fly
she jumped so high
she hurdled the moon.
As she went over
she searched for clover
and when she found none
she said, "I'd as soon
Be in Houston."

Dogs Of Santiago

Do not be a lost dog
in Santiago –
lost dogs in Santiago
trot forever
through the day
and through the night
they trot from shadow into light
and back to shadow
through winter, spring, summer, and fall
looking neither left or right
no longer knowing door from door
insensitive to track or spoor –
never breaking pace.

Be a pit bull
pull carts
run a water wheel
join the canine corps
chase the wolf
or the wild boar
herd cattle or guard sheep
accept the kennel and the leash
if you must
work for police
betray partridge and quail
but do not fail
and become a lost dog
trotting through the streets
of Santiago.

The Camera

I prove life
I prove death

I condemn
I pardon

I animate
I paralyze

I bind
I loosen

I reduce
I enlarge

I fix beauty
I hold ugliness

My eye is everywhere.
I am Tom, peeping

Through the crack in the door,
Under the drawn curtain.

I am the great eye
Looking around the curve of the earth.

I have seen both sides of the moon.
I have seen the depths of the sea.

Cowards turn brave in my beam.
Heroes in action cease fire.

Savage and sage fear me.
"No pictures, please."

Popes and potentates stand
At my call "Hold it" and "Smile."

My power is in deep darkness
In womb of emulsion

Where eggs of silver
Wait for sudden light

No seven days of creation,
No nine months' gestation.

But now and forever. Amen.

Kilroy

Kilroy is gone,
the word is out,
absent without leave
from Vietnam.

Kilroy
who wrote his name
in every can
from Poland to Japan
and places in between
like Sheboygan and Racine
is gone
absent without leave
from Vietnam.

Kilroy
who kept the dice
and stole the ice
out of the BOQ

Kilroy
whose name was good
on every IOU
in World War II
and even in Korea
is gone
absent without leave
from Vietnam.

Kilroy
the unknown soldier
who was the first to land
the last to leave,
with his own hand
has taken his good name
from all the walls
and toilet stalls.

Kilroy
whose name around the world
was like the flag unfurled
has run it down
and left Saigon
and the Mekong
without a hero or a song
and gone
absent without leave
from Vietnam.

Handwriting

The wind blows through your letters.
It draws the dots on *i* 's like smoke
      from east to west.
It tilts the *t* 's but does not bend the *b* 's.
It whispers through the double *s* 's.
It flattens *a* 's and *r* 's.
It puffs up *q* 's and *u* 's.
It sounds most roundly in the *o* 's
and is most gentle with the *m* 's,
especially in your name.
Only the *y* 's, like weathervanes,
point against the wind
to show where it came from.

Tuesday

I am afraid on Tuesday.
Tuesday can be lost
Between Monday and Wednesday,
Chewing each other
Like the blue lips
of the toothless hound.

Wednesday

Today, I will walk all the roads,
All the paths of the world.
I will work at plowing and planting,
Help with harvests.
I will build houses and barns,
Make hinges and handles,
Tables and chairs.
I will untangle yarn,
And watch weavers at work,
Pick apples in old orchards,
Bless abandoned farms,
And all places where hollyhocks
Show that gardens once grew.
I will write a poem,
Before it is Thursday.

No Country For The Young

This is no country for the young.
Vultures prey on living flesh
and eat the skins off kettledrums.
The old refuse to die.

Eyes turn inward, chicken-like,
or stare, unlidded, vague as fish
within a deep and pressuring sea.

At the St. Regis
ice cubes smell of mammoth flesh,
and all the clocks have stopped.
A three-fingered pianist
plays only the black keys
until the dancers fall.
Shadows dare to stand against a sun
veiled by the ash of Hiroshima.

Time is tired of you and me.
It now runs out
like dust
from the broken hourglass.

The young begin too soon
to wait to be the last.
They cover stains of salt and blood
with antimacassars
and watch old curtains disintegrating
from the bottom up.

My Lai Conversation

How old are you, small Vietnamese boy?
Six fingers. Six years.
Why did you carry water to the wounded soldier, now dead?
Your father.
Your father was enemy of free world.
You also now are enemy of free world.
Who told you to carry water to your father?
Your mother!
Your mother is also enemy of free world.
You go into ditch with your mother.
American politician has said,
"It is better to kill you as a boy in the elephant grass
        of Vietnam
Than to have to kill you as a man in the rye grass
        in the USA."
You understand,
It is easier to die
Where you know the names of the birds, the trees
        and the grass
Than in a strange country.
You will be number 128 in the body count for today.
High body count will make the Commander-in-Chief
        of free world much encouraged.
Good-bye, small six-year-old Vietnamese boy, enemy of
        free world.

A Short Book Of Trees

Elm and oak keep decent distances.
Pine and hickory
Crowd and grow in thickets.
Willows are often found
Where they should not be.
They tell of water,
Of old wells and springs,
Both deep and shallow.
Lombardy poplars grow fast in suburbs.
They outlive the sudden people of their planting.
Basswood, like box elders, are found in groves.
They are not much for headlands
And should be kept near bees.
The cottonwood, revered by Indians,
Does not know enough to come in from the cold
Or stay away from river floodlands.
The maple is arrogant.
Now used for rake handles,
It remembers better days
As shaft of lance and spear.
Beech trees are ghostly but truthful.
Their bark will tell
Who loved whom for years.
Apple trees are good
For fruit and holding scythes.
Some trees will not leave home.
Lilacs and sumac stay behind
When houses leave
And lanes are overgrown.

The Fountain

Gently the love laughter
    of water is sounded.
Brightly on wet stones
    light is compounded.

Grace notes sprung
    free flung, faith hung.

Now falling
    down, down, down.

Fountains are futile.
    All fountains fail.

Robert Frost

I

You are an old cow
feeding on overgrazed pasture
of bluegrass and timothy.
You shuttle your head through barbed wire
reaching for sweeter fodder and forbidden weeds.
You drive off critical flies with a slash
of your tail
or more selectively with a forward kick.
Ruminant, you chew a cud of words,
nodding always at questions,
you who have asked yourself all
and answered.

II

You are an old tree,
black maple, on a north slope,
growing clear without shoots or suckers,
like basswood or box elders.
Your knuckled roots hold rocks
deep in the thin soil.
The word sap rises in you,
is drawn off and burned down.
You throw it hot onto the snow.
Pure words form in the cold.
"There you are," you say.
"Now let the green leaves come."

III

You are a Model T painted black.
The choke wire sticks out of the radiator.
The crank hangs in a sling.
Starting you is not easy.
The spark must be set right,
the magneto coils dry.
Your kick can break a man's arm.
On cold days one may have to jack up
one of your hind wheels to get you started.

Once started you are dangerous.
You are always slightly in gear.
Your brakes are marginal.
There is risk in riding with you.
Your fuel tank is under the front seat.
You run on gasoline or on kerosene.
Either can explode.

You are not exactly comfortable.
You have leaf springs but no shock absorbers.
Your tires have inner tubes
and are not puncture proof.
You carry no spare tire,
only tire tools and patching.

Because your fuel system depends on gravity,
not on a vacuum,
you climb steep hills in reverse.
You provide sure passage in spring mud,
have clearance enough for pasture rocks
and for the center ridge of deep rutted roads.

Your fenders carry small boys.
Your running boards are lined with poets.
You get us there.

Nine Horses

Numbered in green paint,
Nine horses in a row.
Sore-footed, spavined,
Heads hung low,
They ignore, as they go,
Cars and lights,
And right of way.

Nobody knew their names.
When busy as the poor, they moved,
Under the hammer of the auctioneer,
Lifting their feet too high,
As the old, dancing in jumps,
Prove they are alive.

Do they remember high plateaus,
Stallions and wild mares with foal,
Percheron meadows, the weight
Of knights in armor, great battles,
And later hunts and races?

The fear in white-eyed blindness
As cataract darkness pours
From the sky ahead of storms,
While heel chains and harness
Irons ring faster than all bells?

Is that half-blind Bucephalus,
Who knew the gentle thighs of Alexander?
And that, Pegasus, with saddle sores
Where once wings sprouted?
And those, the broken-winded ones,
The horses of Antara?

And that one, among them,
With shorter ears, and deeper eyes,
Remembering drumming hooves,
A neck curled, vain with
The mane cresting in the wind,
The sweetness of grass,
The caress of green water
In sliding nostrils,
The fierce movement
Of the loins
And also the taste
Of bread and of wine,
The reaching touch of hands
On the body of a woman?

Does the chest strain to be again
The trunk of man?

Only a cry escapes
Through the fast-growing teeth.
Surprise, surprise,
The last desperate cry,
Of the last centaur.

A Quota On Honey

Now a quota on honey
May seem very funny
To people who talk on TV.
But consider the tree
In need of a bee
To insure it posterity.
The standard Manhattan without a cherry
And no lemon peel for the dry Martini.
The empty hive, the exiled queen,
The disconsolate drone,
The last clover sown,
And in search of one flower
Ladybird wandering
Through the dismal, gray, desolate
Terminal spring.

No Deposit – No Return

Better be wanted dead or alive
Than be a bottle of "no deposit – no return."

The livery horse required a pledge.
The rental car at least a name.
Return postage is guaranteed
On free seed and third-class mail.

Slave ships captained
By men of God left glass beads
On the golden sand.
Bourbon barrels are reused,
Tin cans and old cars
Crushed into cubes
Sent to Japan.

Now leave her here at the nursing home.
She will have company
And continuous care.
No deposit – no return
On the bottle that once knew wine,
The body that once knew love.

For Marcel Marceau

He appears as we look at the dark stage
in a moment of light, the brother of Athena
from the head of Zeus, but dumb.

He holds in his hands, at arm's length, a box.
It is heavy.
The tendons of his elbows stand out.
His biceps knot under his skin.

He is afraid of the box – of what is in it.
He lowers it to the floor.
His back bends
like a pine tree being bowed by weight of vines.

Then he straightens slowly, his muscles easing.
He steps back one step,
looks over his shoulder as if to flee,
or to see if anyone is watching.

Then he kneels,
each joint surrendering in genuflection.
He reaches for the clasp on the box.
He touches it.

He draws his hand back as though it were burned.
He rubs the hand, and slowly reaches again,
takes hold of the clasp. His arm trembles
as though an electric current were passing through it.

He opens the box. Now, an ecstasy of surprise.
Birds fly out.
Others he lifts out in his hands.
He fondles them and tosses them into the air.

He leaps with joy
And then he too flies.
His arms have become wings.
They, he, and the birds turn and soar and dive.

He flies higher than the birds.
He dives more dangerously.
He turns more smoothly.
The birds attack him.

He runs to the box, kneeling again.
He reaches for the birds.
He catches one and puts it in the box.
And another. But now the first one escapes.

He reaches and flails at the birds, more and more slowly.
The mask that is his face changes.
It sags, hanging from the black outline of his eyes
and from the thin curls at his ears.

Now the birds leave.
There is a smell of hunting,
of opened gizzards, of grayness.
He fights at nothing, as in a nightmare.
Now he gets into the box.
Only his hands show, at the last.
They pull down the top, the lock clicks.
The light goes, the dark returns.

My Companion Orders Dinner

On reading a restaurant review

"To begin," she said, "I will have
trivial tripe with alabaster endive,
and three stalks of taut asparagus.
Then the flexible flounder
and two Cote d'Azurs, medium,
with lucid leek and petulant parsnip,
a tensile turnip, a complacent tomato
and a baked preternatural potato.

"I will have the 'plat' plain
and two 'jours,' preferably
Tuesday and Wednesday."
Then, with her head a-tilt
a little like a daffodil,
she said, "To drink
I will have the ambience cold,
and for dessert, a half decor."

Lionesses

I have thought today
Of Edith Sitwell's lioness,
Remembering it is a raging fire
Like the heat of the sun,
The flowering of amber blood and bone,
Rippling of bright muscles like a sea,
The rose prickles of bright claws.

But more.

Much more: of gold and of saffron,
Of a tawny stretching,
A turning of ropes,
The movement of sand
Toward the sea, slower than wind.
And among all of this
Amber, gold, yellow,
Lion-brown eyes, openness.

Lionesses let on a lot.

The Diagonal Dark Path

The diagonal dark path
ran across the park.
False grass beside it grew
and told all that it knew
of everyone who passed,
of every lad and lass
who lay upon it
in thc night.

It ran beneath black walnut trees
that each June deceived
with promises of meat
but in the autumn held but dust
in worm-drilled hulls.

Beyond it stood the public school,
sealed summer sepulcher of heresy.
The coal shute beckoned those
who craved to know
how learning lived
behind locked doors
and dared the cellar dark
and creaking stairs to see
pale blackboards, books
lying like poisoned pigeons
on the floor, husks of flies
sucked dry by spiders
and bees with pollen-laden thighs,
their myriad eyes deceived by glass,
dead or dying on the window sills.

Temptation lurked
in outdoor toilets
padlocked to preserve until September
the janitorial purgation,
sandpapered and planed,
pale spots where once
the facts of life
and who loved whom were told.

On still nights, iron swings
clanged in the calm.
Dead children had come back to play,
old women said.

Each boy at twelve was dared
to walk at night the diagonal path,
not break and run.
Each step no faster than the first
to prove, to prove, he could.

A Fungus Among The Pharaohs

End of the Curse

Dr. Dean of Dublin has determined:
Lord Carnarvon did not die,
As newspapers reported in 1923,
Of a mosquito bite that led to blood poisoning
Which in turn led to pneumonia.

Dr. Dean of Dublin has determined:
It was not the curse of Tutankhamen
That laid his lordship low,
Even though lights in Cairo's Continental Hotel
Did dim, go out at the moment of his death.

Dr. Dean of Dublin has determined:
That stirred from the dry droppings of bats
There was fungus among the Pharaohs
That did in Lord Carnarvon;
Arthur Mace and George Benedite, as well.

Summer Rental

This is my abode until October.
This is a habitable house.
It is a ready house.
Whoever lived here
Left just ahead of me.
They left rubber bands and paper clips,
Stamp holders, letter openers,
And a scale for weighing the mail.

This house has been kept.
There are sachet bags and orange balls
With nutmeg in the drawers.
Summer slipcovers are on the chairs
And summer rugs upon the floors.

The people who lived here
Read Trollope and Defoe.
They left quietly and decently.
Death did not interrupt.
They left generations in cupboards
And in corner closets,
Family silhouettes on the walls
And great-grandfather's sword and cup.

There was no quick sale
Or sudden moving out.
They left only under
The duress of summer.

Margaret

She is very hard to find.
Her eyes are speckled,
Her nose is freckled,
Her hair between chestnut and brown.
Her smile is almost a frown.
She lives in a room full of posters and pictures
With a brindle dog and a calico cat
And a sand-colored gerbil that is really a rat.
Were it not for the windows and door
You could not tell a wall from the ceiling or floor.

She's a trout in the sun,
A fawn in the shade,
A chameleon, ever changing her color.

When asked to use an umbrella, she maintains
"I have had very little trouble with rain."

A Page Of Short Poems

The Lonely:
>   Amputated hands
>   Seeking each other in soft grass.

Ending:
>   I am tired of the moon, she said,
>   Let us go in and turn on the TV.

The Ark:
>   All the animals came to the ark
>   With their mates and their metaphors
>   Save the unicorn, which had no mate,
>   And the aardvarks, which had no metaphors.

Mary:
>   You are gray smoke
>   In a blue vase.

Night after a Dull Day:
>   The waxen day has melted into the sea.
>   The deaf sexton tolls the curfew bell.
>   James Reston chews his cud.
>   Jacob and the Angel
>   Prepare to wrestle to a draw.

The Critic

In a room in an apartment
Where the light breaks back
From other windows
A woman is writing criticism.

Through the closed door
With the one-way spyglass
I hear the drum
Roll of her typewriter.

Now there is silence.
Her hands rise from the keys.
She bites her lip.
Her eyes narrow.

The whole apartment waits.
The city pauses.
The knife of the guillotine holds its notch.

And now words break
In a thunder of keys,
An avalanche of words, behind the door.
Again the woman is writing criticism.

Eaton's Corrasable

To Elizabeth Siebenthall

Who would have expected seventy-three poems in a carton
Of Eaton's corrasable
"With a rag content
Of twenty-five percent,"
And assurances that "you can erase
Without a trace,"
That "errors disappear like magic,"
That "the secret is in the surface."
Seventy-three poems
Including
   The Rise and Fall of the Goat
   The Color of Purple
   Blue Lake

The secret is not in the surface
Or in the rag content
Of twenty-five percent
In the seventy-three poems
In the carton of Eaton's corrasable.

Your Garbage Man

I am your garbage man.
Near the furnace
In the apartment basement
I am sitting in your old Victorian chair.

1 know more than you think.
People die slowly,
A little bit at a time.
In some cases dying takes a lifetime.

Not everything you throw away
Goes straight to the crusher or to the incinerator,
Or to the scow, headed for the Atlantic.
Some things I keep for myself.
Some I sell.
Some I give to relatives or friends
Or to the Goodwill Industries.

Your old brown pants are mine now.
I can tell from them how you walked.
I am waiting for the coat and vest.

Things are not going well for you.
Your shoes are resoled.
Your shirt collars are turned.
There are spots on your old neckties.
Your grade of whiskey has gone down.
You are drinking house brands.
I find empty Geritol and Grecian Formula
Bottles in your trash.

According to the Environmental Protection Agency
Each American uses twenty-eight tons
Of materials a year.

I carry you away many times
Before the mortician does his job.

When the body dies
There is loss of weight.
What is lost then is carried
By Charon, the boatman.

Park Lane Hotel, Toledo, Ohio

Newspaper notice: "The Park Lane Hotel closed today."

The Park Lane Hotel, Toledo, Ohio.
Conrad Hilton never slept there
or left his bedside reader.
Not even the Gideons have left their book.

Room two hundred and four.
Like other rooms, a bed,
a chest of drawers, a chair,
and a desk, bookcase,
with three shelves of books,
unlike the books in any other room.

For fiction lovers:
Faithful Shirley (copyright 1892, 1893, and 1899).
Also, *Lost, a Pearle,* and *Virgie's Inheritance,*
all by Mrs. George Sheldon.

The Main Chance, 1903, by Merideth Nicholson,
dedicated to D.K.N., "who," we are assured in
the foreword, "will remember and understand."

Woman of Spain, by Scott O'Dell.
This book was formerly the property of
the Toledo Home for the Hard of Hearing.

Battling Love and Faith, 1902,
by Mary V. Allen.

The Daughters of Anderson Crow, 1907,
by George Barr McCutcheon.

And for lovers of nonfiction:
The Memoirs of Barras, Member of the Directorate,
18th Fructidor to 18th Brumaire,
Year V to Year VIII, published in 1896.

Modern Eloquence, in V Volumes, published in 1903.
The standard for selection was "style," which may
be defined as "proper words in proper place."

Volume I of the *Life of Charles Dickens,* 1905,
by John Forster (ex libris John O'Day, of Boston).

Volume IV of *Health and Strength,*
by John Nelson Goltra, M.D., 1917 to 1925.
"Written to teach by games and sports, the great
lessons of life."

Volume II of the *Works of Shakespeare,*
The Kenneth Roberts Reader of 1945,
and Volumes VII and VIII
of the new *International Encyclopedia,*
published in 1927, from Didymus to Foraker
(Joseph Benson Foraker), governor and senator
from Ohio, who, according to the last entry, in
May 1914 announced that he would run again
for the Senate in order to clear himself of charges.

There is no report in Volume VIII as to whether
Foraker won or lost or cleared his name. It may
be in Volume IX, in some other room.

There were four pictures in the room:
one of the three Graces,
one of a lady with two wolfhounds,
and two prints, of wild flowers
of September and of October, annotated.

There is a new Hilton in Toledo.

The Blue Guitarist

You do not play things as they are
When you play upon the blue guitar.
Now play the truth,
The Bishop cried. People said, Yea, Yea, Amen.
And the judge said, Play,
And the bailiff, too,
And they called in the sheriff
And the National Guard.

The fingerman sighed
And drew a deep, deep breath.
Now he laid the guitar across his knees.
He tuned each string to a perfect pitch.
Then he bowed his head to the work ahead.
He said, I will play things on the blue guitar
Exactly as they are.

He played it high and he played it low.
He played it fast and he played it slow.
He played it round and he played it square.
He played it well done and he played it rare.
He played it thin and he played it fat.
He played it sharp and he played it flat.
He played it loose and he played it tight.
He played it left and he played it right.
He played it new and he played it old.
He played it hot and he played it cold.
He played it crooked and he played it straight.
He played it early and he played it late.

Then the Bishop cried,
Oh, play no more on the blue guitar,
No one wants to hear things as they are.
And the people said, Yea, Yea, Amen,
And the judge, and the bailiff,
The sheriff and the National Guard.

Then the fingerman raised
His hand from the strings
And the blood dripped down from his fingertips.
He eyed the crowd with a terrible look
And he struck a chord never heard before
As he broke the neck of the blue guitar.

Orthodox Convention

Morning

The sons of Levi now decree
The interchangeability
Of plastic casings
And the guts of goats
For kosher sausage.

Afternoon

The sons of Levi on rented skates
Cut the ice in figure eights
While Sarahs and Jezabels and Ruths
Walk the lobby in new pants suits.

Evening

Since crows cry havoc in all seasons,
Why didn't Noah know
Better than to send a crow
To see if spring had come.

"Roaches Take Over New York City Buses"

– New York Times

Roaches are not afraid of time –
They live in electric clocks.
Roaches are not afraid of space –
They live in cracks.
So why be surprised to find them on buses?
They are not afraid of motion.
Moreover, there is roaches' work to be done on buses.
Removing crumbs,
Keeping the engines clean of grease.
And survival fare in plastic seat covers.

Roaches go where they are needed.
And as a spokesman for the Transit Co. said,
"It's not a problem unique to buses.
Once a roach settles in, he's as much at home
On a city bus as in a Park Avenue apartment."

"We urge any passenger who sees a roach,"
He added, "to get the number of the bus
And call us."

Einstein had nothing to say to roaches.

House Movers

House movers, among men, are not to be blest.
The house that has been moved is never at rest,
Jacked up on girders and rollers,
Pulled down the street, against the wishes
Of trees and telephone wires.

Its new foundations are never right,
Too high or too low.
The trees are all strangers,
Distant and nervous.
They shade the wrong places.
Neighboring houses frown,
Their windows stare in the wrong places,
There are blank walls where
There should be windows and doors.

And at the old site,
Houses left behind worry.
Why did it leave without notice?
Did it have something to hide?
Which of us will be next?
Better to have torn it down
Or let it die.

Elm trees, in the yard, lean the wrong way.
The willows hang round the abandoned well.
The sumac decently cover
The wound of the open cellar,
Filled with old mattresses,
Tin cans, and barbed wire.
Lilacs slowly close the unused road.

House movers are not to be blest.

Admiral Radford Crosses The Continental Divide

Admiral Radford crosses the Continental Divide
asleep at thirty-two thousand feet.
He dreams of blue water, of his ships
moving above the mountains of the Pacific.
He dreams of coordinates,
of trajectories, of parabolas,
of the slant-eyed mariners
set against his straight and hooded look,
their ships built
with plans stolen from the Germans,
the steel of their hulls
from the planned waste of America.
He will strike at dawn,
guns at the ready.

The plane lands. His wife
stirs him awake.
No smart salutes, no piping through salt spray,
no descent of uncertain iron stairs.
The accordion tube of the airport
reaches for him.
He is helped into his wheelchair.
His wife pushes him out of his dreams.

Reflections On J. L.

She was different among the women
in the drawing rooms of London,
among titled widows, mistresses, and wives.
She was different among the men,
dandied dukes and earls and lords
who publicly proposed, and poets
who spoke at length of Guinness.

"She is Scotch," they said, "and haughty."

She walked among tables and chairs
thigh free as in heather,
leaning a little as into a wind,
clearer eyed, looking through
planes of air to farther hills.

Her hands were strong with the knowledge
of linen and wool, and the leap of the loom.
She wore the colors of moor and of heath
and her hair was true raven.

Much truth is in the roots
under light-footed walking
among scant flowers.

"She is Scotch," they said, "and haughty."

London

Steady flow of cabs and clerks.
Careful about small things,
Dates of births and deaths,
Of foundings and of failings.
Of titles, qualifications, and credentials.
Ltd. Inc. Esq.
Shirtmakers to dead kings,
Milliners to headless queens,
Vintners to alcoholic princes,
Tobacconists to prince consorts,
Money changers for Germans or French,
Lending it for War or Peace.
Modulated, impartial. A city of service,
Keeping time and standards.

Mouse

Ah, he was there. I heard
The burr of his scurrying between the studdings,
The high cries of his little lust,
The shrieks of his small fears.

Ah, he was there. I saw
His shadow among the shadows
Circling the reach of faint light.

Now, in the bottom drawer,
Following my nose, I find his remains -
Five whiskers, the claws, and the end of his tail.

He who of all the beasts,
Except the swallow, is most unbiddable,
According to Pliny.

His body, unfit for food,
And causing oblivion if eaten,
According to Porta.

A "verie ravenour or greedigut"
Considering his "bigness,"
According to John Maplet (1567).

He lived most intently
His twoscore months and ten
His heart beating
Five hundred strokes to the minute,
Thirty thousand to the hour.

A fierce interior life.
His blood pressure beyond measure.
His liver waxing and waning
With the mood of the moon,
According to Aelian.

Listening, touching, squeaking,
Tasting, watching, but beyond
All of these, smelling.

Rampant, he was, among odors,
His nose twitching, his whiskers shaking,
His olfactory faculties at full speed.

Now he has left five whiskers,
The claws, and the end of his tail.
And ah, yes, a roomful of odors.

A room filled at his death with his life.
Drawn through small nostrils, extracted,
Compacted, in the silk sack of his body,
The essences of cheese, of mold, of dry bread
Now released.

If we had but let him smell better–
Rose leaves, tarragon, mint, and wild thyme–
How sweet and sublime
Would the death odors be
To go with the five whiskers,
The claws, and the end of his tail.

The Great Green Suit

There once was a patriot named Cuneen
Who had a suit of unusual sheen
Combining mold, and mist, and shamrock green.

It was, without doubt, the greatest of tweeds.
Its woof was wool, its warp of Irish reeds.

It stood alone, without hanger or board.
It had strength to withstand night stick and sword.

It was loose at the shoulder for fighting the British.
It was full in the trouser for running in ditches.

Its color was such that for hiding in heather
There was nothing better, and as for the weather,

It was fine in the sun but much better in rain,
For it repelled water, and scarce showed a stain.

It was so marvelous in its variety
It could serve, in a pinch, as a hair shirt for piety.

Then a woman's derision
Brought about a decision

To send the suit to the cleaner to have it made lighter
And then to the tailor to have it made tighter.

When the call came on the first moonlit night,
Kept from the fight and also from flight
Because the suit was too tight, Cuneen,

Concealed in a thicket so as not to be seen,
Was found by the smell of the kerosene.

On the very next day at the moment of dawn
They hanged him on the courthouse lawn.

But they honored at death his last request
And he wore the green suit to his final rest.

To Austin Clarke

William Butler Yeats is dead.
Patrick Kavanaugh gone to his reward.
Old poets, young poets, poets,
Honor Austin Clarke.

He walks alone in Ireland,
Black hat, muffler, greatcoat,
Threadbare buttonholes,
Pale eyes smiling, white hair
Drifting down like smoke in a heavy day.
It is left to him
To be the tongue of Ireland.
Listen to him at the last.

"I've no quarrel with the poets.
I've outlived nearly all my old friends.
Most of them died of drink.
I was saved by a weak stomach.
Many of the younger ones have gone to America
To teach, to live. I've stayed here.

"I've no quarrel with the Church.
The Archbishop is an able man.
There are many able men in the Church.
There must be for it to last.

"I've no quarrel with the government.
Poets are not censored in Ireland.
Playwrights, novelists, yes.
Not poets. Indifference, perhaps.
Irish Broadcasting treats me well.
They pay me even when I don't go on.

"Once as a boy
I climbed the wall at Coole Park.
Through the trees, I saw Yeats, walking.
It was wonderful.

"Poets don't know much, but they try.
They try every way; blind as bats
And deaf as well, they fly.
They carve stone with bone,
Form steel with sand.
They fight like small boys
With their eyes shut.
Crying before they are hurt, but brave."

Men In Vows

I sing today
In praise of oath-bound men,
Harnessed and held in vows
To patient or impatient wives,
To flags, to ships, perhaps to God.
No battering at the gates,
No fierce assault,
No beating of high air,
No condor eye cast only downward,
No hawks dive through bluing air,
No blood on beak or talon,
No red-tipped feather floats
Down from their air to write
Fear on the earth.
Well within the walls, the hulls,
The cells, they brace
Against the centrifuge,
Holding the center while others
Swing in wider gyres
And beat against the outer limitations
Of our powers.
On wax-held wings, wary of the sun,
They circle on updrafts from low hills
And from flat fields.
Slowly up near life
And gently down to death.

Courage At Sixty

Now it is certain.
There is no magic stone,
No secret to be found.
One must go
With the mind's winnowed learning.
No more than the child's handhold
On the willows bending over the lake,
On the sumac roots at the cliff edge.
Ignorance is checked,
Betrayals scratched.
The coat has been hung on the peg,
The cigar laid on the table edge,
The cue chosen and chalked,
The balls set for the final break.
All cards drawn,
All bets called.
The dice, warm as blood in the hand,
Shaken for the last cast.
The glove has been thrown to the ground,
The last choice of weapons made.

A book for one thought.
A poem for one line.
A line for one word.

"Broken things are powerful."
Things about to break are stronger still.
The last shot from the brittle bow is truest.

Tumbleweed

The tumbleweed never gets
a decent burial.
Not even in a common grave
with leaves and straw,
never matted down
and turned to mulch.

But driven by the wind
it moves in uneven starts and stops,
like Indians being driven to
less hospitable ground.
A dried and arid spirit, swirling
with Dante's rejected souls.

The small seeds lost in flight,
abandoned like children of the poor.
(No phoenix here, no new plant
out of the death of old.)
Spread-eagled, at last,
against wire fence,
it slowly turns to dust.

Ground Fog & Night

A cloud is subtly woven over the field.
Day and night together beget the cataract film.
It holds, while the earth, with its burden
Of brush and of trees,
Of houses and steeples, sinks slowly.

Day songs die and night birds' songs
Are dampened by the fog.
Crescendos of cicadas cross
The prairies of the night
And then are gone in silence like the bison.
Ruminant stomachs yield their cuds
And tree frogs
Fall into green sleep.
Spiders lying upside down
Like Michelangelo on his back
Make a ceiling between themselves and God.
Plants rid themselves of death
Spawned in them by the sun.
Burrowing beasts live on as before.
Shrews and moles shelter
In their dark world the hoard
Stolen from the light.

Now owl and vermin do contest.
No winners from the day.
Men in air-conditioned rooms set clocks
Against the night and wait for dawn.
No sign of God is left above the fog.
Only the red-eyed tower stands
To tell of life
Below.

To Robert Lowell

Poet of purity and of parsimony
using one sense at a time, sparingly.
Salt-bleaching white the whiteness of light,
straining the hemp, not nylon line,
scraping the wood to bare the silk grain.

Searching in attics and sheds,
of life, salvaging shards and scraps,
of truth, parts of dead poets,
pieces of gods.

Myopic, in storms, you cross
the bridge of the faulted rocks,
double agent of doubt, smuggler of truth.

Poet-Priest of the bitter sacrament,
what is behind the door in man's house,
what is beneath the cross in God's house?
Look through your less dark glass,
daring as much for man as for God.

James Dickey

Why do you shout of things not thought,
or if thought, not spoken?
Palpable crier of man,
animal, earth, machine.

Are you a prophet with scorched lips,
sent, to add to the light
and heat of the sun, a voice
in the cock's curdled cry,
and also to speak for the moon?

What is your power
to bear up the girl
we dropped in the well
of the sky, and prepare
her for death on your own
sky drowning terms?

What is your gift
to inspirit tractors and trucks,
to bear fire, the bright blooming napalm
back from the jungle, to leave
in our back yard, clinging
and caught, like a hound
in hog wire?

What is your license to drag us
to the May-day barn scourging,
we who would rather stand off and listen,
to hold us, while lasers of light
from roof board holes
thin slice our souls?

What is your writ to whisper us
back to dusty shelves
where man and his animal
face their beginning and ending
in a clouded jar of alcohol?

Never content, forever seeing, smelling
hearing, tasting, feeling, talking, revering.
We give thanks for the violent man.

Lament Of An Aging Politician

The Dream of Gerontion is
                    my dream
and Lowell's self-salted
night sweat, wet, flannel,
                    my morning's
shoulder shroud.

Now, far-sighted I see the distant
                            danger.
Beyond the coffin confines of
                    telephone booths,
my arms stretch to read, in vain.

Stubbornness and penicillin hold
the aged above me.
My metaphors grow cold and old,
My enemies, both young and bold.

I have left Act I, for involution
and Act II. There mired in
                    complexity
I cannot write Act III.

A Baker's Dozen Of Short Poems

1. The Nearsighted Poet

Writing poetry
with one's glasses on
raises questions that go beyond
the normal limits bards patrol.

2. Lilacs

Lilacs are hard to move.
They are Victorian women:
all elbows, hat pins,
petticoats, and corset stays.

3. Sound

Horses' hooves fall
on frozen ground
like stones upon
a coffin top.

4. The Four Elements

Canvas for those who die in water;
wool for those who go by fire;
silk for those who go to death through air;
linen for all claimed by earth.

5. Tanagers

Scarlet tanagers,
like women
afraid of their own beauty,
try to fly out of their colors.

6. Riot Time, Washington, D.C. 1964

Today, in rain,
black men and women
sell flowers wrapped in papers
telling of yesterday's riots.

7. The Seal

Except for its fur and its feel
the seal is very much like an eel.
And, if it had tusks,
it might pass for a walrus.

8. Boredom

Said the fish,
"I wish I could close my eyes.
The view from the bottom
is boring."

9. Bloodhounds

Bloodhounds know
no statute of limitations.

10. Pigeons

Pigeons and dentists
dip their heads
and look askance.

11. Castrati

The castrati
sang the cantata
soprano a capella
to please Il Papa.

12. Pine Trees

Love, like the pine tree,
will not grow
in its own litter
unless the whole
is purged by fire.

13. The Cave

The cave does not call.
It listens.

The cave does not go out.
It waits.

The cave does not use.
It keeps
bones, stone tools,
and scratchings on its walls.

Gossip Columnist

Couturier marked, save for straps that show
At the shoulder and a slip below
And rippling like a spent snakeskin
A fold of nylon at the shin,
She does the Australian crawl
Into the center of the hall.

There beneath the chandeliers
She tests the sonar of her ears,
Through lids half-closed against the light
Her eager eyes search left and right.

Birds sense the cat and do not sing.
Chickens cackle incoherence,
Field mice squeak to silence
Under the hawk's dark wing.

When she enters voices drop.
As she approaches conversations stop.
Undeterred and unabashed
She gathers gossip as she goes,
Scattering spores of rumor by the way
For fungal harvest another day.

Then Clotho, Lachesis, Atropos,
A trinity, she combines,
Spinning, allotting, cutting the lines,
Fierce, yet fawning, just short of hate,
She writes a column, just short of fate.

Wherever I travel Greece keeps wounding me.
They call the ship which travels Agony 937.
George Seferis

Jumping Ship

I signed on the *Constitution*
for 67 days, 46 ports,
a good ship
with wall to wall carpets,
clean, with Goren for bridge,
full of joy and forgetfulness
according to Isbrandtsen,
more than seaworthy

Ignoring the Atlantic waves
nodding to the swells off Africa
somewhat too large
for the Mediterranean,
certainly for the Aegean,
drawing too much for the pier,
we stood off the coast.

Out of your land
from the ship *Agony 937*,
out of your language, in translation
you boarded violently,
crying of Greece, George Seferis

With the wounds of Greece
you have wounded us.
You have wounded us with the deep sound
of women crying out of centuries,
and with the shallow silence
of the buried reed.

You have wounded us with the sharp fear
of the broken oar, marking the grave
on the shore,
and with the blunt despair
of the harbors without ships.

You have wounded us with the white
of the almond trees,
and with the black
of the burnt out villages.

You have wounded us with the sweetness
of the pomegranate,
and with the bitterness
of the salt sea.

You have wounded us
with the weightless walking of children,
and with the heaviness of the marble heads
and of the great stones.

You have wounded us unto death
and unto life.

With eleven ports to go
I am jumping ship
to sign on *Agony 937*.

Bicycle Rider

(to Mary)

Teeth bare to the wind
Knuckle white grip on handle bars
You push the pedals of no return,
Let loose new motion and speed.
The earth turns with the multiplied
Force of your wheels.
Do not look back.
Feet light on the brake
Ride the bicycle of your will
Down the spine of the world,
Ahead of your time, into life.
I will not say
Go slow.

On The Death Of Vernon Watkins While Playing Tennis

Beneath the earth's uneven crust
no root will thrust into your mold.
Your body will not change to dust.
Like cool reflections in a pool
long-green, upside down trees will grow.
Their leaves and branches will enfold
your fair form and bear slow
light to you and moving air.

Vernon Watkins, near wanderer,
your voice careful as shadows,
a night wind among dry oats,
your voice, a gloved hand turning
gulls on updrafts above
the reaching estuary.

You held your place where the morning
wind stops and turns back to the sea.
You walked in the narrow space
where waters stand divided
after the moon lets go,
before the ebbing tide.
You promised violets
out of winter's frost.
Took the gold of day
into the blackness of the mine.
The sullen dark you raised
to the mystery of light.

Fearless, you looked into
the single eye of Dylan,
the multiple cold, honorable eye of Yeats,
Accountant of life, patient acolyte
turning the pages for bad priests,
the word, a eucharist, gentle,
upon your tongue.

Vernon, of the hills and heather,
Poor bird who knew the air,
why did you risk the cage?
Poor fish who knew the sea,
why did you dare the net?
Poor beast who knew both grass and thorn,
why would you run on macadam?
Rectangles, rules, a net,
advantage, game, and set.

"The game is done, I've won, I've won
Quoth she and whistles thrice."
Tennis was not your game.
Dressed in divers colors, Vernon,
why did you play the woman
in white?

I Would Be

I would be with you first in high places
There – where love and all is tentative
in that lean space where birch trees tense against
thin winds, and scant grass prys
among the ice ground glacial stones.

I would be with you, too,
where spruce spring separate,
touching only at arms length
in accidental motion, as one looks (the other
looks away,)
knuckle on cheekbone and back
of hand to back of hand, not more.

And then go on to openness and shade
of elm and oak, in confidence and fear,
into the no longer free fields, tempting
the thistle, taunting the thorn, knowing
the good of the floating flower of flax,
the joy of the wind random in a field of
ripening rye, the hot fertility
of corn in June, sterility of stubble,
the burden of the meadow
where heavy hay lies
bleeding in slashed rows, composed
as men fallen in more human wars,
with limbs left and identity for a day.

And then at end go
down to the last aridity of sand,
flat yet curving, under the flat yet curving
face of the sea. Curve under curve, eternity,
all made real by our seeing and saying
together, Yes, Yes.

Rapid City

Sumac singed in the slant
sun, tumble weed and thistle, scant
green gone, in the fear of old
thigh bones, brittle in cold.
On every hill a last Indian sits,
looking straight west, through saffron slits,
reading his blood, paler and paler, exile,
while parched snakes wait for the first
thin dew to slake their day-old thirst.
The coyote cries in the sudden night
and from stars dead a million years, light,
on the yellow leaves of cotton-wood,
shows that under the iron bridge
                a black river is, and flows.

Rome

City of beauty - positive and negative
of bone and flesh - of bottles and wine
continuing - always digging out
another deeper century.
Purpled by bishops
reddened by popes
air thinned by blessings
under a pall of prayers,
bright by day,
brighter by night in light
brought back from all the torches of the past
like that from stars burned out
layered in beauty of women
perfected as conqueror's choices
Etruscan and Roman - Greek, Gaul
Shopkeepers, street cleaners
clerks, accountants,
rose
Caesar's army in disguise,
wait in the Roman December
for the Roman Spring.

Rome,
always leading captives
through your streets,
today in your best beauty,
winter yellow and brown,
you lead me.

Grant Park, Chicago

Morning sun on the pale lake,
on plastic helmets, on August
leaves of elm, on grass,
on boys and girls in sleeping bags,
curled in question marks.

Asking
the answer to the question
of the song and of the guitar
to the question of the fountain,
of the bell and of the red balloon
to the question of the blue kite
of the flowers and of the girl's
brown hair in the wind.

There are no answers
in this park, said the captain
of the guard.

Then give us our questions
say the boys and girls.

The guitar is smashed,
the tongue gone from the bell,
all kites have fallen, to the ground
or caught in trees
and telephone wires
like St. Andrew, crucified,
hang upside down.
The balloons are broken
flowers faded in the night
fountains have been drained
no hair blows in the wind
no one sings.

Three men in the dawn
with hooks and spears,
three men
in olive drab gathered
all questions into burlap bags.
They are gone –

There are no questions
in this park
said the captain
of the guard.

There are only true facts
in this park
said the captain
of the guard.

Helen did not go to Troy.
The Red Sea never parted.
Leander wore water wings.
Roland did not blow his horn.
Leonidas fled the pass.
Robert McNamara reads Kafka
Kirkegaard and Yeats – and he said on April 20, 1966,
"The total number of tanks in Latin America is 974,
This is 60 percent as many as a single country,
Bulgaria, has."

There are only true facts
in this park
said the captain
of the guard.

Quiet Waters

There are quiet waters
where a berry dropped
by a bird flying
starts ripples that
from the center of the pond
spread in concentrics, dying
in silence at the feet of the blue reeds.
I now know where these waters are.

The Road From Emmaus

I walked alone from Emmaus
met a friendly company on the road,
heard soft voices,
felt the warmth of love
and passed on.

Dulles Airport

Detached by Saarinen or God
from all coordinates,
it sits like a gull upon water
defying the subtle Archimedean rule.

The earth flows without displacement.
In this the only measured space of the world,
we come each a half two hundred yards
from shadow to form
from form to person, to meet
within the green range of each other's sight.

There at the center point, at midnight,
no arrivals, or departures scheduled
ticket sellers and stewardesses sleep,
planes and pilots are released.

Into this innocence of light,
not one eye of the myriad-eyed mankind
dares look. Let us dance, slowly turning.
We are seen by the immodest,
unlidded, unblinking, snaked-eyed electric beam.
The door opens out. Not driven
but drawn by darkness, we go
naked into the immeasurable night.

Willow In A Tamarack Swamp

There in the savage orange of autumn tamarack
rusted spikes reeling the slanted, last
of the northern day, down
into the black
root waters,
among the least trees in that least land
in the darkened death camp
of the tribe of trees
I saw you.
green gold willow, arched and graced,
among spines and angled limbs.
captive? queen?
all lost light from the smothering swamp,
alone, you bear back.

Place Of Promise

I hunt for the white doe
in winter dusk – snow
falling in the forest of birch
and of beech. I know
my search must end.
I am in the place of promise
with no track or trace.

Whiteness alone, not light
holds back the punctual night.
I have walked through spring
white against green,
of anemone, laurel and thorn,
searched the pale mist of plum,
put my hands in the tangled skein
of wild cherry.

In my passing, I scattered
the scant white of summer,
the wind-drift of willow and thistle.
My knees knew the white
of daisies and asters
that spin in the wind
in the fall.
I waded thigh deep
in the dry foam of milkweed.

The white of all seasons now
trod under my feet
lies in a casque of sleet.
Still, quiet, in this clearing,
I stand, testing, in trust,
the word, on a cold crust
of water.

Right Of Way

Here you find no counted seeds
Or calculated crops
Only the most wanted weeds
Nettles, great thistles, and burdocks
With exiles and expatriates from pot and box
Gypsy plants, despising rows
Alien corn, unhelped by hoes
Asters, lupine, sumac, and thorn –
Stranger plants, of no fame,
Which country Adams across
The fence, look at
As of forbidden knowledge
And refuse to name.

Free and not free
In this sanctuary
I reached, seeking you, in want
All the joints of my arm parted
And then drew back a hand
Bled by the rasp of harsh grass
With a reed made
Of that bitter blade
I blew three notes
And thought of how
If you were there
I would hold your hair
Against the wind, and hear through it
The harping of all the wild songs
Of Ireland.

The Gleaner

Be a gleaner of time
Claim what runs through the hourglass
When no one watches
What is counted by clocks, ticking
When no one listens
Save remnants
From the cutting room of day
End pieces from the loom of night
Brand and hold
Unmarked, maverick minutes
Salvage time left derelict
By those who despair of light
Yet fear the dark
Steal only from sleep
And from eternity
Of which time no one dares ask
What? or Where?

Equinox, September 1967

Summer ended Friday
at midnight in doubt
between rain and fog
half way through the equinox.

The great wheel of the seasons
had risen to apogee
and stood in balance
defying time's grasping forward pull.

Like a bird held
by hard winds
or a movie reversed
it fell back toward spring.

But then came over, slowly
down falling, inexorable
on the side of autumn
its force against me.

I called. You did not come.
The winter will be longer.

Equinox, March 1968

Whose foot is on the treadle
That turns the burning stars
Has spun the whole world half way round
Since last I called
Come down. Come down.

The stars that in September
Looked through the mournful rain
Now set their sight again
Upon a world half night, half light.

Men of distant years have said
That much depends on change of seasons
On solstices and equinox
And they have given reasons.

I disagree.
Too much turns on inadvertence
Or what seems to be
An accident of hand or knee
A chance sunrise
A glance of eyes
Whether the wind blows
Which way the river flows
And on other things that come and go
Without regard for season
Or for reason.

But just in case
They may be right,
On this strange night
That marks the end of winter's fall
For lifting help towards spring
Again, to you, I call.

Dies Illa

In that day the sun
will come, unsung,
its voice choked
in the black cock's throat.
Arthritic scythes will lie
beside the ripened rye
and folded flails, in vain
wait for the threshers and for grain.
Saddled horses will drift
unridden through the land.
In the forest only
hollow trees will stand.
On windless seas sails will hang slack.
At the forge all color will be black
The water wheel will
in the mill stand still.
Tops will not spin. No ball
will bounce. All kites will fall.
Swallows will not dart, nor hawk
soar. The mocking bird will mock
neither song nor silence.

I will be he who waits
by the gray sea with Yeats,
empty, hollow, wasted, cold,
more silent than unmocked silence.
Yet the weight of the nail
is better to bear
than the torment of pins
and the locked white chair.

Early Spring

Black is the color
of the early spring
Black birds sit bravely
on weak reeds and old
corn stalks and scold
Brown birds hide
in brush and balks
Black cats are bold
Crouched on fence posts
they balance the world
Calico cats are cowardly
They cringe and crawl in winter grass
Black roosters crow
and take full strides
White roosters mince
and are asthmatic
Black horses prance and stamp
in frozen pastures
Pale horses tremble in the cold
and are arthritic
Black cows come out of barns
wintered well and sleek
Brindle cows are gaunt and weak
Black bulls are brash. They bellow
and rattle barn stalls with knobby heads
Red bulls complain and are phlegmatic
Ploughed lands lie
beside gray stubble, black
as velvet, threatening
to turn green.

The Clock

(to Ellen)

The clock passes the Time –
Doesn't it, my daddy –
Wisdom of the world asked
in four year old brown-eyed
certainty – Time –
encompassing without pause
unmarked duration
continuum without commas.

We strike it to measure,
water drops, sand, notched wheels,
impulses and escaping ions.
No answer yet, my darling.

All come to this knowledge –
You are the only clock,
passing the Time.

The Day Time Began

Our days were yellow and green.
we marked the seasons with respect,
but spring was ours. We were shoots
and sprouts, and greenings.
We heard the first word
that fish were running in the creek.
Secretive we went with men into sheds
for torches and tridents
for nets and traps.
We shared the wildness of that week,
in men and fish. First fruits
after the winter. Dried meat gone,
the pork barrel holding only brine.
Bank clerks came out in skins,
teachers in loin clouts,
while game wardens drove in darkened cars,
watching the vagrant flares
beside the fish mad streams, or crouched
at home to see who came and went,
holding their peace,
surprised by violence.

We were spendthrift of time.
A day was not too much to spend
to find a willow right for a whistle
to blow the greenest sound the world
has ever heard.
Another day to search the oak and hickory thickets,
geometry and experience run together
to choose the fork, fit
for a sling.

Whole days long we pursued the spotted frogs
and dared the curse of newts and toads.
New adams, unhurried, pure, we checked the names
given by the old.
Some things we found well titled
blood-root for sight
skunks for smell
crab apple for taste
yarrow for sound
mallow for touch.
Some we found named ill, too little or too much
or in a foreign tongue.
These we challenged with new names.

Space was our preoccupation,
infinity, not eternity our concern.
We were strong bent on counting,
the railroad ties, so many to a mile,
the telephone poles, the cars that passed,
marking our growth against the door frames.

The sky was a kite,
I flew it on a string, winding
it in to see its blue, again
to count the whirling swallows,
and read the patterned scroll of blackbirds turning,
to check the markings of the hawk,
and then letting it out to the end
of the last pinched inch of
string, in the vise of thumb and finger.

One day the string broke.
The kite fled over the shoulder of the world,
but reluctantly, reaching back in great lunges
as lost kites do, or as a girl running
in a reversed movie, as at each arched step, the earth
set free, leaps forward, catching
her farther back,
the treadmill doubly betraying,
remote and more remote.

Now I lie on a west facing hill in October.
The dragging string having circled the world, the universe,
crosses my hand in the grass. I do not grasp it.
It brushes my closed eyes, I do not open.
That world is no longer mine, but for remembrance.
Space ended then, and time began.

Saturday

Saturday is a whale
It swallows people
for three days
Saturday is the sphinx
It has a locked secret
Saturday is Mona Lisa
Its smile is inscrutable
Saturday is a Castro convertible
It is closed all day
Saturday holds its breath
Saturday, if it comes,
could last forever.

Sunday

Today
the river does not threaten the reed
nor wind frighten the willow tree,
Mist is not a burden on the moor
nor frost a weight on clover.
Air is unscarred by lancing wings,
The sound of bells
does not oppress the land,
Tide and running waters lean
against each other without complaint.
All things that should,
touch, without hurt or harm
It is Sunday.

Communion

Gentle the deer with solicitude
Solace them with salt
Comfort them with apples
Prepare them for the rectitude
Of Man who will come
A stranger with the unfamiliar gun.
The watcher calls. In trust the head
                              turns.
Between the antlers St. Hubert's cross
                              burns.
No conversion today – but quick shot.
The buck falls to his knees
In decent genuflection to death.
                    The doe flees.
He is not dead. He will arise.
In three weeks, the head
Will look from the wall
But with changed eyes.

But what of the body of swiftness
And litheness. Oh. Witness?
Ground heart and muscle,
Intestinal cased, tied with gristle,
The sausage sacrament of communion.
So that all may be one
Under the transplanted eyes
of the watcher.

10 Commandments

1.   Do not watch a woman
        reading a menu
2.   Do not rest in light let through
        where a branch breaking refused
        to hold a child's swing
3.   Be silent in a mill
        when the water wheel and the
        grinding stones are still
4.   Do not relight a candle
        whose flame has drowned
        in its own excess of wax
5.   Walk through ruins only in the
        dark or at noon
        leave no shadow
6.   Do not look long on a harbor
        from which all ships are gone
7.   Speak always as though children
        were listening
8.   Trust the grass
9.   Listen to wind and
        running waters
10.   Never shoot through the
        strings of the still harp

In A Chinese Mode

Five drops of rain
fell on a stone.

The first one said
 I have been ice.
 The sky is green before the hail.

The second said
 I was once the farthest flung
 at the Trianon.
 Fountains are futile.
 All fountains fail.

The third one said
 women like to walk in rain.
 I have known the dark tangles
 of a lady's hair.

The fourth one said
 I have been a tear.
 I have tasted salt.

The fifth one said
 I am new water
 made of lightning and air.

The Snails Of St. Paul de Vence

All summer long
in fields beyond
St. Paul de Vence
they watch the flowers
flame and fade.

The gold of Van Gogh
the silver of Cezanne
gone, earth-bound they wait
to see a second coming, late
pale green and yellow
August butterflies
against vague skies.

No petals fall
from these. All
colors disappear
out of the snail's near
sight.

It is September.
Now, the snails remember
these fields were meant
for flowers and slow,
single-footed, climb
on twice-used, spent,
uncertain, shallow
rooted stems, to shine,
pearl, blue, and white
in that slant light,
a third, unpromised coming.

Three Bad Signs

The first Bad Sign is this:
"Green River Ordinance Enforced Here.
Peddlers Not Allowed."

This is a clean, safe town.
No one can just come round
With ribbons and bright thread
Or new books to be read.
This is an established place.
We have accepted patterns in lace,
And ban itinerant vendors of new forms
                                                    and whirls,
All things that turn the heads of girls.
We are not narrow, but we live with care.
Gypsies, hawkers and minstrels are right
                                                    for a fair.
But transient peddlers, nuisances, we say
From Green River must be kept away.
Traveling preachers, actors with a play,
Can pass through, but may not stay.
Phoenicians, Jews, men of Venice –
Know that this is the home of Kiwanis.
All you who have been round the world
                                                    to find
Beauty in small things: read our sign
And move on.

The second Bad Sign is this:
"Mixed Drinks."

"Mixed Drinks."
What mystery blinks
As in the thin blood of the neon sign
The uncertain hearts of the customers
Are tested there in the window.
Embolism after embolism, repeating.
Mixed drinks, between the art movie
And the Reasonable Rates Hotel.
Mixed drinks are class,
Each requires a different glass.
Mixed drink is manhattan red
Between the adult movie and the
                              unmade bed.
Mixed drink is daiquiri green
Between the gospel mission and the sheen
Of hair oil on the rose planted paper.
Mixed drink is forgiveness
Between the vicarious sin
And the half-empty bottle of gin.
Mixed drink is remembrance between
                              unshaded
40-watt bulbs hung from the ceiling,
Between the light a man cannot live by,
And the better darkness.
"Mixed Drinks" is the sign of contradiction.

The third Bad Sign is this:
"We Serve All Faiths."

We serve all faiths:
We the morticians.
Tobias is out, he has had it.
We do not bury the dead.
Not, He died, was buried and after three
                              days arose.
But He died, was revived, and after three
                          days was buried alive.
This is our scripture.
Do not disturb the established practitioner.
Do not disturb the traditional mortician,
Giving fans to the church, for hot days,
Dropping a calendar at the nursing home,
A pamphlet in the hospital waiting room,
An ad in the testimonial brochure at the
                              retirement banquet.
Promising the right music, the artificial grass.
We bury faith of all kinds.
Foreverness does not come easily.
The rates should be higher.

The Heron

The heron comes before the light
Has quite distinguished day from night.
Where he stands all things turn gray.
His yellow eye rebukes the sun.
Pricked by his beak, all colors run
Through his one leg into the bay.
All day, disdained, the dismal fishes swim
About that one deceiving reed
And flout the warning line
That runs from his sun-moved shadow
To the point of death.

Why does the heron wait
Alone, controlled, celibate?
Simon Stylites on his rod
Looking for the weakening of God,
The executioner who prays
A day before he slays.
When at last the sun slanted
Beneath his clouded breast has changed
All things to gold, delayed,
The answer comes.

The heron strikes and kills his wish.
For he eats only golden fish.
And that same fish, mirrored
In the heron's avid eyes,
Sees himself as golden and dies
in that belief. Both fish and bird
By the same sun, at end, betrayed.

Ares

god, Ares
is not dead.
he lives,
where blood and water mix
in tropic rains.
N, NNE, or S
or W, no compass –
only mad roosters
tail down on twisted vanes
point to the wind
of the falling sky
the helicopter wind
that blows straight down
flattening the elephant grass
to show small bodies crawling
at the roots, or dead
and larger ones
in the edged shade, to be counted
for the Pentagon, and
for the New York Times.

ideologies can make a war
last long and go far
ideologies do not have boundaries
cannot be shown on maps
before and after
or even on a globe
as meridian, parallel
or papal line of demarcation.

what is the line between
Moslem and Jew
Christian and Infidel
Catholic and Huguenot
with St. Bartholomew waiting
on the calendar for his day

to come and go?
what map can choose between cropped heads
and hairy ones?
what globe affirm
"better dead than red"
"better red than dead"?
ideologies do not bleed
they only blood the world.

mathematical wars go farther.
they run on ratios
of kill and over-kill
from one to x
and to infinity.
we are bigger, one to two
we are better, one to three
death is the measure

it's one of us to four
of them, of eight to two
depending on your
point of view.
12 to 3
means victory
12 to 5 forbodes defeat.
these ratios stand
sustainèd
by haruspex and IBM.
we can kill all of you
three times
and you kill all of us
but once and a half – the game
is prisoner's base, and we
are fresh on you
with new technology.

we sleep well
but worry some. We know
that you would kill us twice
if you could, and not leave
that second death half done.
we are unsure
that even three times killed
you might not spring up whole.

snakes close again
and cats do, it is true
have nine lives. Why
not the same for you?
no one knows about third comings
we all wait for the second, which
may be bypassed
in the new arithmetic.
or which, when it comes
may look like a first
and be denied.

the best war, if war must be
is one for Helen
or for Aquitaine.
no computation stands
and all the programmed lights
flash
and burn slowly down to dark
when one man says
I will die
not twice, or three times over
but my one first life, and last
lay down for this my space
my place, my love.

Grass

grass is very troublesome to God and man
it comes in such variety
and does not hold tracks
like mud or even sand.

Silence

the mocking bird
does not mock the silence
of other birds. its silence
is its own.

Vietnam Message

We will take our corrugated steel
out of the land of thatched huts.

We will take our tanks
out of the land of the water buffalo.

We will take our napalm and flame throwers
out of the land that scarcely knows
the use of matches.

We will take our helicopters
out of the land of colored birds
and butterflies.

We will give back your villages and fields
your small and willing women.

We will leave you your small joys
and smaller troubles.

We will trust you to your gods,
some blind, some many-handed.

Are You Running With Me Jesus?

"people are running . . ." Parade Magazine

Billy Graham wherever he is,
George Romney every day,
Senator Proxmire to the Capitol and home again.

      Are you running with me Jesus,
      Asks the Reverend Malcolm Boyd.

      May I ask the same?

      I'm not matching my stride
      With Billy Graham's by the Clyde.
      I'm not going for distance
      With the Senator's persistence.
      I'm not trying to win a race
      Even at George Romney's pace.

      I'm an existential runner,
      Indifferent to space.
      I'm running here in place.

      Wall to wall unending,
      The treadmill carpet flows.
      Baseboard to baseboard unchanging,

      From the looms of Mohawk.
      As I run against the clock,
      Are you running with me Jesus,
      Or not?

The Tamarack

The tamarack tree is the saddest tree of all;
it is the first tree to invade the swamp,
and when it makes the soil dry enough,
the other trees come and kill it.
It is very much abused.
It cannot grow in shade,
is put upon by parasite growths,
witches' broom and the dwarf mistletoe.

The Maple Tree

The maple tree that night
Without a wind or rain
Let go its leaves
Because its time had come.
Brown veined, spotted,
Like old hands, fluttering in blessing,
They fell upon my head
And shoulders, and then
Down to the quiet at my feet.
I stood, and stood
Until the tree was bare
And have told no one
But you that I was there.

Recessional

(from the installation of a Bishop, 1970)

The Program
  "The Cross of New York
  The Bishop of New York
  attended by the Coadjutor and the Suffragan
  The Canons of the Cathedral Church

A Cross
The Bishops in their order
The Choir

A Cross
The Chancellor and the President
  of the Standing Committee
The Standing Committee
The Trustees of the Cathedral
The Officers of the Diocese
The Representatives of other Religious Bodies
  and Academic Institutions

The Clergy of the Diocese
The Clergy of other Dioceses
The Members of Religious Orders
The Seminarians of the Diocese."

The Instruction
  "The Processions will retire in direct Seniority,
    proceeding the length of the Cathedral,
    and leaving by the Great Bronze Doors."

The Action
  and so they did go
  with dignity
  out through the Great Bronze Doors to
  Amsterdam Avenue.

The Aardvark

I am alone
in the land of the aardvarks.
I am walking west
all the aardvarks are going east.
Aardvarks cannot look and listen
at the same time.
They are listening, now, listening
to the sound of the marching feet
of the termites they are going to eat.
The termites are behind me.
They are choice termites.
They have grown fat
on the dead wood of the tree of knowledge.
Even if the aardvarks were looking
they could not see me.
I am wearing red and green.
Their world is empty of red and green
and of pink and purple and
Roman brown. Their eyes do not narrow
in the light or widen in the dark.
They see only gray
both night and day.
They push through the red earth.
It parts before them but does
not close behind.
With their long tongues
they speak a thin language
I do not understand.
Aardvarks think always of soft food
because they have no gizzards.
I am looking for you.

In Praise Of Three Men Of Ireland And Of Their Wives

This, then, is a poem of praise in the manner of Forgaille,
the Chief poet of Ireland, who for his writing of Columcille
The Speckled Salmon the Boyne, the High Saint of the Gael,
was given heaven.

It is a story, not a little one, of three men of Ireland
and of their wives, all called to wander the world, without
fixed home or shelter, in the service of the Irish government
and of the IRISH TIMES.

It is of gray-eyed Dermot of Leitrim, with the name of
one who was no respecter of kings, and of his wife, Maeve,
named after the great queen, restrained, even now, by
the weight of the ever growing cairn of Knocknarea, she
whom kings and heroes feared, but, who, herself, feared
no man.

It is of blue-eyed Conor, of Antrim, named after many
kings, He of the sharpest weapon, the pen, forged and
hammered by the same demon who made Concubar's sword blade.
And of his wife, Shanna, gifted with tongues, valued as
that which is brought from the furthermost lands.

(We now move for the names into the Christian era)

It is of Brendan, with the mixed eyes of Kerry, named
after saint and sailor, who, some said, looked always
to the West. And of Margaret, his wife, so burdened with
virtue as to need two saints of her name for support:
Margaret of Antioch, one of the fourteen helpers of God,
her specialty aiding those with backache, a common
ailment among the Irish, and Margaret of Scotland, a Queen,
there five centuries before the coming of the Presbyterians.

This is a story, not to be sung to a harp with even one
string broken. It is not to be satisfied with the praise
of one District of Ireland, but of all Districts, or with
the acclaim of only Leitrim, and Antrim, and Kerry, but
with the acclaim of all counties.

It is not separable praise that is to be given to these.
For the wives are all, and each fair and comely, and
wise and of strength. And the men, such as were the three
sons of Usnach, of whom it was said that a good word
spoken for one was spoken of all. So is it of Dermot,
and Conor, and Brendan.

Three that would never tell a lie.
Three that would cause no one vexation.
Three that to be with was never wearisome.
Three darlings of the women of Breton.
Three hawks of Slieve Duileen.
Three lions of the Hill of Cave.
Three equal pupils of Conall Cearnach.
Three skilled in the handling of falcons.
Three that held the leashes of the three hounds.
Three that were not good at paying homage.

Now, and if, distinction is to be made among them, it
is only of that which can be made among the equals of
the "Three in One," as incarnate in Columcille.

In Dermot, we have Columcille, the dun of the book
of the law, the diplomat, skilled in settling of disputes,
Dermot, warned by Aengus, not to go into a tree to hide
if the tree has but one trunk; nor to enter a cave that
has but one opening, or land on an island with but one harbor.

In Conor, Columcille, the teller of words, thief of the
scriptures, plagiarist of God's works.

In Brendan, Columcille, master of politics and of the
sea, wise in both, understanding seasons and storms,
knowing the course of the moon, and watchful of its
race with the branching sun: wise in the ways of the sea,
of its running and of its changes.

I now end with the words of Forgaille, who when he ended
his poem in praise of Columcille, declared. "It is a
great shaping and a great finish I have given to these
words, and I cannot make any praise beyond this."

Nor can I, for the Gallaghers, and O'Clerys, and the Scannells.

On the occasion of the return of the Scannells, to Ireland,
August 30, 1993.

The Public Man

He walks, even in daylight, with arms outstretched.
Fish-like he shies at shadows
His own, following him, nose to ground
Like a blind bloodhound.

Gray fish swim through
the cavities of his skull.
He feeds the sterile cows, the steers of no desire,
With the mast of the bitter grapes.

He closes his eyes to fire flies,
And his own light
Which once burned bright
Is yellow tallow.

His words rise, like water,
Twice used, from the cistern pump.
And then go out in a wavering line
As beagles run, intent on catching rabbits.

Like a gull, crying with tired voice,
He looks back, often, into the fog.
Each night he holds his head of stone between his hands.
As his elbows slowly sink through the table top.

Borysthenes And Katie

"Jim-Bill will bury that horse," said Clifton Clark
Of Katie, the old white mare.
No one in the country store did dare
Question or challenge Clifton's remark.

"She'll never be trucked to a slaughter house
To be shot, and skinned, and ground into meal,
Or having died a natural death, to a rendering plant,
To be boiled, and melted and distilled
To the essence of horse and beyond.
She'll not be fed to the hounds in the kennel
Or stripped of her hide and left in the pasture
For hogs and vultures and crows.
She'll not be cremated with brush fire and oil
Nor stuffed, moth-proofed and hung on a frame
Like Lee's horse, Traveler, of Civil War fame.

A horse like her is hard to find
And not to be treated as ordinary kind.
She never fell, or threw man, woman, or child.
Yet she set the pace for every ride.
She would Jump what other horses refused,
But none but a fool, horse or man,
Would try when she turned aside."

She'll be buried there on the west hillside
Whole of body, with unmarked hide
Not crowded or jammed in a ditch,
But laid on her side in an ample grave,
Neck extended, legs stretched for a joyful run
With Borysthenes, Hadrian's hunter
Who some 2000 years ago, his epitaph states,
"Galloped through plains
And marshy meadows
Past old Etruscan barrows
And chased the Pannonian boars.
Lived long, and then
With his legs unblemished
Met his fate, appointed,
And in the field was buried."

The Proud And Careless Words

At the end of three score years and ten
The Biblical time allotted to men
The New Republic marks the date
And pauses to evaluate.

Encouraged to note that at one-ninety-five
The Old Republic did survive
Presidential change from George to Ronnie
The leap from Adams to Bush as V. P.

The New Republic, like the Old, has stood the years
Despite confusion, and doubts and fears
Since Lippman and Croly and Walter Weyl
Rudyard and Hacket and Philip Litell
Sustained by high principles, interest income and oil
And profit from reapers that lightened men's toil
To come to the day of Marty, and Richard and Morton
Of Charles, of Michael, of Ann and Leon
With occasional help in the ultimate now
From the Kristol (ball) Irving, and the Irving (know) Howe.
All dependent in part on the sewing machine
Which fact does in no way their thinking demean.

Now, if your great worries are economic
And micro and macro do not make you sick
Or if you are deep into "real politic"
Then listen to Michael, or Morton, or Rick.

If you seek to unravel South American snarls
Or master the mystery of Mid-Eastern quarrels
You need only look to Marty, or Leon, or Charles.

If art and culture are your concern
And you're desperate not knowing where you should turn
You'll find help in the words of Charles, Ann, and Leon.

If you're one who long followed dear Richard Lee Strout
The well-known, anonymous T.R.B.
Worry no more, for the secret is out,
T.R.B. lives on in Michael Kinsley.

When The New Republic comes again
To the end of its second three score and ten
And its search for heroes and saints goes on
Its friends will stand as we do now
And toast the memory of Kristol and Howe
Of Charles, of Hendrick, of Mort, and of Ann,
Of Marty, of Michael, and of Leon

Whose proud and careless words will live on
When all this heavy history is gone.

Fawn Hall Among The Antinomians

"And I can type," she boldly said
With a toss of her carefully tousled locks,
"Smuggle papers and run the Xerox.
And I know how and what to shred.
For I am an Antinomian."

She never turned brave Ollie's head
For he honored his oaths, he said,
Unless directed by some authority
Which gave lying a higher priority,
Sustained, as he was by the Fifth and immunity
And basic Antinomian impunity.

Admirable, Admiral John Poindexter
Came with his lawyer, his pipe,
And his clerical wife.
Certain he knew what the President thought
He wrought a deniable, plausible plot
Never thinking that he'd be caught
In his Antinomian coup d' etat.

The Reed And The Stump

"A reed, shaken by the wind, are you,
"Halton." said the prefect, Montagu.

"What you say," said Halton, "may be true,
"But what kind of wind is it, Montagu?"

"Is it a bitter wind, and does it blow
"From the left or the right? That you should know."

"Oh! And should I," said Montagu, "Now
"Would you tell me, Halton, why and how?"

"Enough of that," said Halton
"It is time we were getting on."

"The next question is: Where does the reed stand?
"Is it in the salt water off the strand?"

"Is it shaking there in the shrouding fog?
"Or is it rooted beneath the black waters of a high bog?"

"And what is more. Has it ever crossed your mind,
"Montagu, as to what the reed does for the wind,

"That without the reed, the wind would be mute
"As a harp is without strings, or a lute."

"It has crossed my mind many times that you,
"Halton, are a reed shaken by the wind." said Montagu

"And you, Montagu, are a stump, the butt
"Of the tree of knowledge," said Halton. "Cut,

"Shredded, glued, Montagu
"To insulate us from much that is true."

"Moreover, you are cut so close to the ground
"That you glean from moving air, not a sound."

"You nourish no green leaves, but give life
"Only to fungi and light fearing termite."

40 years later

"Where," said Montagu, on the bus to the aeroplane
"Do you go, Halton, you, in your crush hat and tweedy look?"
"I go to Oxford," said Halton, "John Chrysostom, to explain.
"And You, Montagu, with your cassock and book?"
"I travel farther with one of the tours
"That go, on schedule, from Dublin to Lourdes."

As Halton stepped down from the bus, "I'll pray
"For you there," he heard Montagu say.

"And, I," said Halton, as he shook in the wind that blew
From Dublin Bay, "I'll sing for you, Montagu."

A Letter To Marianne Moore

(in tribute to Joseph Grucci))

Come quickly to your city.
All the boats at the piers
are quiet, waiting for you.
Only their flags and pennants move
and those gently as tongues whispering
you down from the sky.
The horns and whistles all are silent,
so that you can hear our softer call.

The Staten Island Ferry leaves no wake
All the waters are still
mirrors waiting for your face.
If another looks, they erase
with quick ripples and regret.

The bridges are bowed,
waiting, and the tunnels call.
The gargoyles hold their stern faces,
but like children waiting to open
presents, threaten to smile.

The lions at the library, one can see
in peripheral vision, twitch their tails,
eager to follow you down the street.
We have promised them your coming
to quiet them.

Everyone knows that there are brown butter-
flies in your hair, and agates
and small mirrors in your purse
and words.

Come quickly to your city.

To Katie Louhheim

on the publication of
With or Without Roses

Poet of unclear spaces
  Drawing lines and pointing
  But leaving free the sacred place.

Poet of the high ridges
  Running their edges, sharp
        above the dark valleys
  But offering neither roads or bridges

Poet of what is left to fill
  with hope and love
  When men stop short for ignorance
        or want of will.

"Words have color. The way we see colors determines words."
Steven Pinker, Semanticist

When That Time Came

When that time came
To name all things of earth and sky
And give them colors.

The coyote first cried "yellow."
The cock crowed "red!"
The loon, alone, laughed "blue."

The fox barked "black."
Tree frogs whispered "green."
The wolf howled "purple."

Pigs squealed "pink."
Rabbits shrieked "white."
Bulls bellowed "brown."

Mules brayed "gray."
Cats snarled "orange."
And Adam said:

"Now language has begun."

The Smuggler Speaks

I am not a salesman
I am not a manufacturer's agent.
I am not a priest of God.

I am not above or below.
I am not before or after.
I am in-between.

I deal in contradictions.
I exchange truth for falsehood.
Good for bad, love for hate.

I make no simple trades.
I buy and sell gold and counterfeit.
I market loyalty and treachery.

I do not work in darkness.
I do not work in the light
But in early and late gray.

I represent popes and people
Kings.and commoners
Saints and sinners.

I do not travel over-burdened
I do not travel without burden
But moderately laden.

I have no one country
I am not without a country
I have many countries

Marie Teresa is my empress
See her there in fat profile
On our coinage.

The Hapsburgs were against borders
So am I.
I am a poet.

Tom Halton Among The Homoousions

Of his three score years and ten
Seventy will not come again
So if you're keeping Biblical score
That doesn't leave him any more.

But students of the scriptures know
There's always one more verse to go,
And that no true scholar can find rest
Until he's checked the last-found palimpsest.

Whereas the septuagenarian textual measure,
Acknowledging the decline of bodily function
Defines the end of sensual pleasure,
Punishment for earlier excess, to be eased by Extreme Unction

The psalmist offers ten years more
To those with strength to bear pain and labor
And spend the added years refining creeds,
Their failing sight perusing screeds,

To discover who said what first
Who identified the earliest atheist,
Why Augustine spurned the Manichaes
And who were the bishops of Dead Seas.

True doctors of patristics
Are not shaken by contradictions or statistics.
Nor do they fear to tread
In places even angels dread.

Some stand with Irenaeus and his views
That martyrdom's the sure way to salvation.
Others opt for Athanasius and choose
To make their way by killing heretic and pagan.

Some dare to ask "Was Leo really number one?"
As was declared at Chalcedon
And draw the line between Homoiousion and Homoousion,
The difference being a vowel or preposition.

Some endorse the grammatical assertion by the Great,
That the subject is the predicate. (or vice versa)
And accept the conflation of three Mary's into one,
Now carried on the calendar as The Magdalen.

Today we start with Halton, a ten-year wait
For one more wide-eyed Arab spelunker
To dance out of a dry Judean sepulcher
With a scroll, ultimate, or perhaps, penultimate,

Revealing that all persons born in County Cavan
Have a head start on the road to heaven.

Mollie

I know that you will not come back
Not answer to my call or whistle
Not come even at your pleasure
As was your way.
Yet, I will leave your "good dog" pad and dish
Beside the kitchen sink, a while.
Your rawhide bone beneath a chair
The cans of dog food on the shelf
Your favorite ball, which you
hid in the boxwood hedge.
I'll listen in the early morning light,
For your muted huff, not quite a bark,
Suggesting you be let out.
And lie in half-sleep until
I hear your harplike
Single scratch upon the screen
To signal you had answered nature's call
Made your accustomed rounds
Checked the limits of the grounds,
For trace of groundhogs, raccoons, even bears
And now returned intent on sleep
On bed, or rug, or floor
depending on your mood.
And if not answered,
Lie down in silent protest
Against my failure to respond
And to show resentment of the
Indifference of the stolid door.

I will not yet remove
The mist of dog hair
From your favorite chair.
Not yet discard the frazzled frisbee
You could catch, making plays,
Going away, like Willie Mays.
But having proved your skill
Refused to fetch;
Let retrievers tire themselves
In repetitious runs, you seemed to say.
You would run figure eights,
Disdaining simple circles
Jump hedges just for sport.
Eat holes in woolen blankets
But leave untouched
the silk or satin bindings.
Herd sheep and cattle
Spurn running rabbits and deer,
That would not play your game.

You swam with ducks
And walked among wild geese.
Ate Tums but not Rolaids,
You knew no dog-like shame.
And died by no dog's disease at end,
But by one that also lays its claim on men.

For Eugene McCarthy

I love you so . . . Gone? Who will swear
you wouldn't have done good to the
country, that fulfillment wouldn't have
done good to you – the father, as Freud
says: you? We've so little faith that anyone
ever makes anything better – the same and
less – or that ambition ever makes the
ambitious; the state lifts us, we cannot
change the state – all was yours though,
lining down the balls for hours, freedom in
the hollow bowling alley: crack of the glove,
the boys . . . Picking a quarrel with
you is like picking the petals of the
daisies – the game, the passing crowds, the
rapid young still brand your hand with
sunflects . . . coldly willing to smash the
ball past those who bought the park.

        Robert Lowell
        July 6, 1968

Index of Titles